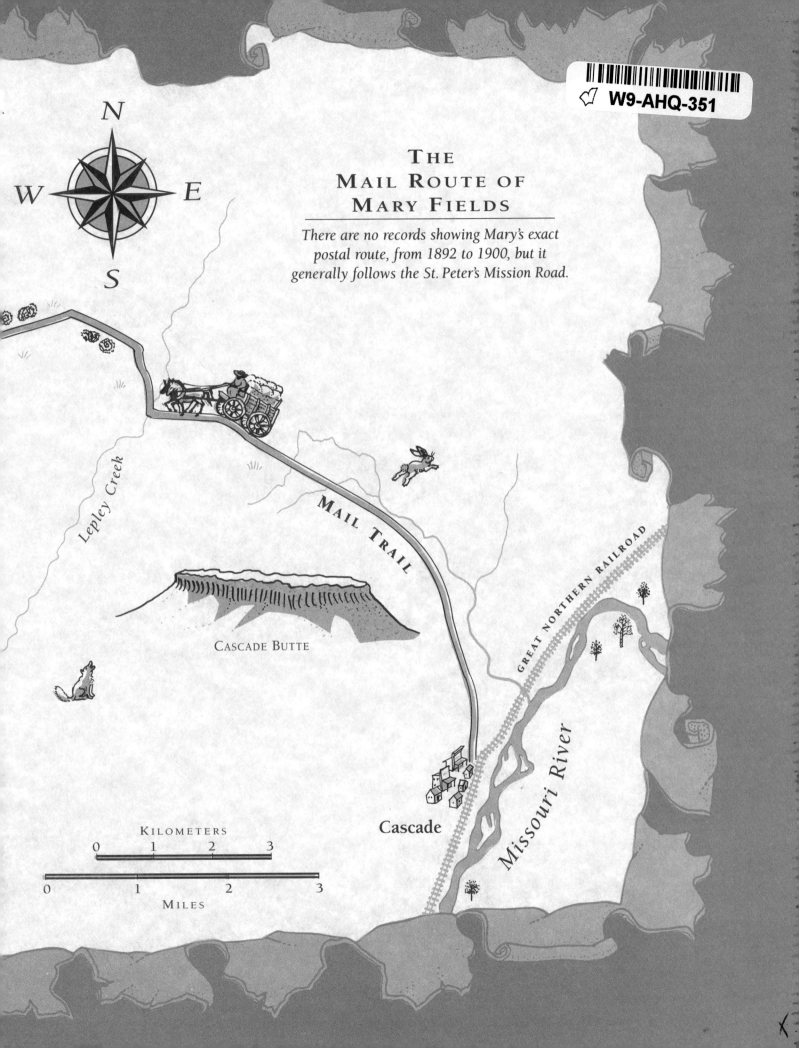

THE MAIL ROUTE OF MARY FIELDS

There are no records showing Mary's exact postal route, from 1892 to 1900, but it generally follows the St. Peter's Mission Road.

N
W E
S

Lepley Creek

MAIL TRAIL

CASCADE BUTTE

GREAT NORTHERN RAILROAD

Cascade

Missouri River

KILOMETERS
0   1   2   3

0   1   2   3
MILES

THE STORY OF
STAGECOACH
MARY FIELDS

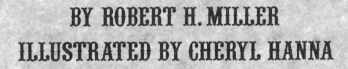

BY ROBERT H. MILLER
ILLUSTRATED BY CHERYL HANNA

Silver Press

*To my sisters, Margaurite and Princine, your zeal
and spirit characterize the black pioneer
woman   RHM*

*For my mother—another rebel. You always
cheered for the Indians   CIH*

*To Ms. Toni Trent Parker, for suggesting this western series for young
children. Thank you. Robert H. Miller.*

Text copyright © 1995 Robert H. Miller
Illustrations copyright © 1995 Cheryl Hanna
Map copyright © 1995 Claudia Carlson
All rights reserved, including the right of reproduction in whole or in part
in any form.
Published by Silver Press, Paramount Publishing, 250 James Street,
Morristown, New Jersey 07960
Printed in the United States of America.
10 9 8 7 6 5 4 3 2 1

Library of Congress Cataloging-in-Publication Data
Miller, Robert H. (Robert Henry), 1944–
The story of "Stagecoach" Mary Fields / by Robert H. Miller ; illustrated by
Cheryl Hanna.
p.   cm. — (Stories of the forgotten West)
ISBN 0-382-24394-3 (SC)   ISBN 0-382-24399-4 (JHC)
ISBN 0-382-24390-0 (LSB)
1. Fields, Mary, b. ca. 1832. 2. Postal service—Montana—Letter carriers—
Biography—Juvenile literature. 3. Coach drivers—Montana—Biography—
Juvenile literature. 4. Women pioneers—Montana—Biography—Juvenile
literature. 5. Afro-American pioneers—Montana—Biography—Juvenile
literature. 6. Frontier and pioneer life—Montana—Juvenile literature.
[1. Fields, Mary, b. ca. 1832. 2. Postal service—Letter carriers. 3. Pioneers.
4. Afro-Americans—Biography. 5. Women—Biography. 6. Frontier and
pioneer life.] I. Hanna, Cheryl, ill. II. Title. III. Series.
HE5385.F53M55   1994   383'.143—dc20   [B]   93-46286
CIP AC

Among the unsung heroes of the West were the people who delivered the mail. In 1860, prior to the development of the Transcontinental Railroad and the invention of the telegraph, an experiment called the Pony Express was put into operation between St. Joseph, Missouri, and Sacramento, California. In this system, riders carried and delivered the mail on the backs of swift-riding ponies. While faster forms of transportation and communication soon made the Pony Express obsolete, the stagecoach remained a prevalent form of carrying the mail from town to town. One particular route—from Cascade, Montana, to St. Peter's Mission, just seventeen miles away— was perhaps the most famous route of all. It had as its rider the first African American woman ever to carry the United States mail. She was sixty years old when she got the job. Her name was Mary Fields.

Back in the days when the West was just as wild as a mustang
stallion, there lived a woman as strong and willful as the land
itself. Mary Fields was born in Hickman County, Tennessee,
around 1832. Though she was born a slave, Mary had a wish
as big as Texas to be free.

By the time she was five years old, Mary could outrun children twice her size. Her daddy tried to teach her all about planting crops. But Mary would just as soon eat a live toad as do her chores!

But riding horses—that was something! Mary and the master's daughter, Dolly Dunn, liked to race down to the river. Pretty soon, the girls became good friends.

Time passed quickly on the plantation. Soon the master's daughter moved away. Mary grew to be a big, strong woman. She learned to read and write. And when she was just about all grown-up, Mary took to smoking cigars!

When the Civil War ended in 1865, Mary Fields became a free woman. But Mary had worked for the Dunns all her life. They treated her like family. Now they were happy to pay her

wages for her work. So Mary decided to stay put. But she was restless. Day after day, she waited and hoped for something new to happen.

Then one day Mary got a letter. Her childhood friend Dolly was now a nun. She wanted Mary to join her at St. Peter's Mission, near Cascade, Montana. Mary dropped everything and prepared to join her friend.

A lot of time had passed since Mary and Dolly ran wild
around the Dunn plantation. They were no longer girls, but
grown women. Mary stood tall, wearing Western clothes and
a six-shooter strapped to her waist.

Dolly, who was now called Sister Amadeus, welcomed her
with open arms.

She showed Mary around the mission, which was old and in need of repair. Mary settled in right away. Soon she got to work. Mary helped the men, moving stones and fixing everything in sight.

Soon, Mary became the workers' boss. But one man didn't take too kindly to a black woman telling him what to do.

One day, Mary was shouting orders to the men. But this new fella didn't pay her any mind.

"Okay, Mister Sack O' Lard, get a move on," Mary said.

The other men laughed. But this new fella didn't.

"Since when does a slave boss a white man?" he said in an angry tone of voice.

"Ain't no slaves here, mister. Now I said *move* it."

What happened next surprised everyone!

The new fella walked up to Mary, swung, and knocked her down.

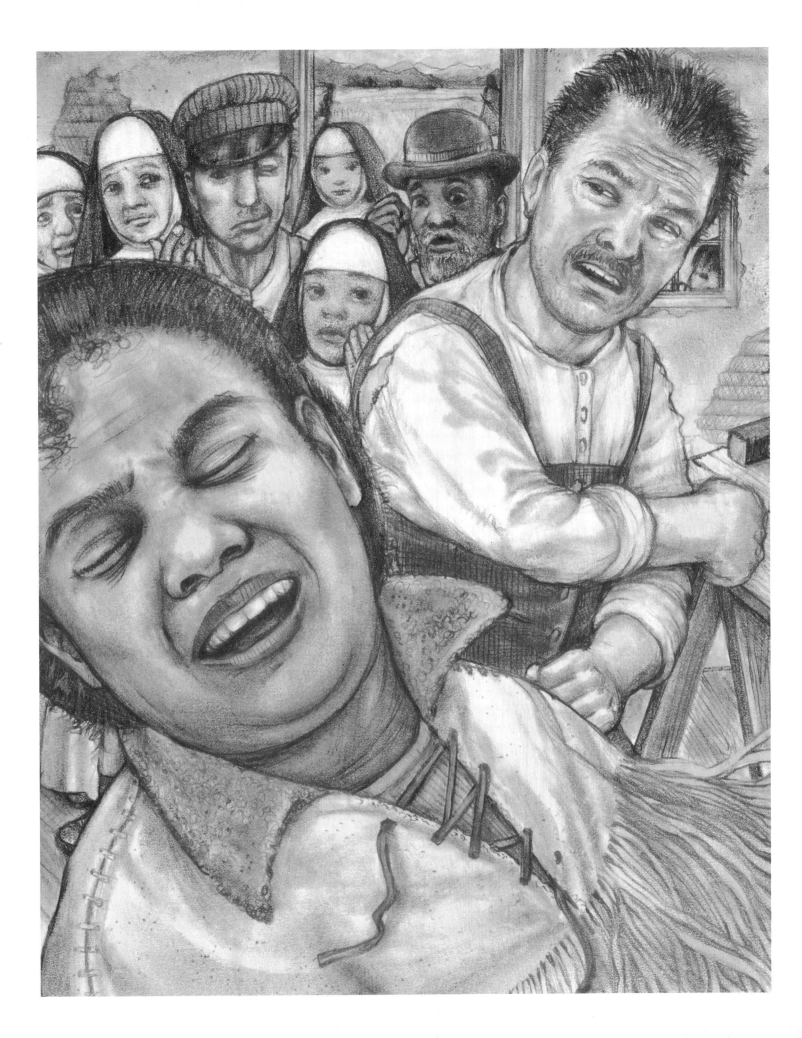

Mary jumped to her feet just as quickly as she hit the ground.
Growing up on the plantation, she had learned to use a gun.
"Strap on your guns, mister, and meet me in the street," she said.

Quicker than a squirrel can blink, the man went for his
six-shooter. But Mary was faster. She fired three shots, and the
varmint keeled over.

Then Mary walked over to the barnyard and started feeding
the chickens.

"I beat him fair and square," she said, turning to the workers.
"No man lays a hand on me."

The story of the gunfight spread across the territory. Soon it got back to the bishop.

"That black woman has become a nuisance," he said to Sister Amadeus. "She has to go!"

The sister knew she couldn't change the bishop's mind. But she didn't want to lose Mary. That night, she thought and prayed about how to keep Mary at the mission.

Next morning, Sister Amadeus remembered that the United States Mail Service was opening a new route between Cascade, Montana and St. Peter's Mission.

The new route was going to be tough. It followed a scrawny mountain trail that passed through badlands crawling with outlaws. Only the strongest and most experienced riders even thought about taking the job.

At least forty riders stood before the depot on the day that
Mary rode into town. She jumped off her chestnut-brown
stallion. With a rifle in one hand and a cigar between her teeth,
Mary strutted up the steps of the depot.

"I'm here for the driver's job," she said. "Who's the boss of
this place?"

A stout little man came out of the depot. "I'm doing the
hiring," he said. "Who wants to know?"

Mary stepped right up. "I do. Where can I sign up?"

The depot manager looked at her carefully. "You ride horses, ma'am?" he asked.

"I can drive a team of six horses better than anyone here," Mary said.

"If that's true, you've got the job. But first you've got to hitch up them horses." The manager pointed to the livery stable where the horses were kept.

Well, faster than you can say giddyap, Mary had those horses hitched! With one crack of her whip, they took off like they'd been stung by a swarm of yellow jackets.

"Move it!" she hollered.

By the time Mary brought the horses to a stop, the depot manager had made up his mind. He hired Mary on the spot. And that's how Mary Fields became the first black woman ever to carry the United States mail.

Delivering the mail wasn't easy. More than once, Mary tangled with bandits. But nothing kept Mary from delivering the mail on time. If a bandit got too close, Mary would switch the reins to one hand, draw her six-shooter, and fire, all the while going at full speed. She soon became known as Stagecoach Mary Fields.

Once, during one of those bad Montana winters, the snow slowed down her horses to a dead stop. Mary just loaded the mail on her back, grabbed her rifle, and walked ten miles to the depot. And would you believe it, the mail got there on time—as usual.

Another time, Mary was racing back to the mission along familiar trails. She was taking every shortcut she knew. Sister Amadeus had taken sick and needed special care. The mission's food supply was also running short, so Mary loaded up the wagon with supplies.

It was nearly night. Coming down the top of a hill, Mary didn't see a dry gully below. As her wagon hit it, there was a sound like rolling thunder. Supplies flew everywhere.

Quickly Mary calmed her horses. She knew that darkness would soon set in. Working fast, she got almost all the supplies back on the wagon. But by now night had crept in like a thief. Wolves and coyotes were howling.

Mary sat out the night with only her rifle for company. "Get back, you rascals," she shouted and fired into the darkness whenever the wolves got too close.

When daylight came, Mary was off to the mission. Sister Amadeus started feeling better once she saw Mary.

"I'm so glad you're back safely," she whispered.

"Don't you worry 'bout a thing," Mary answered. "I'm here now."

Within days, she had nursed her best friend back to health.

After eight years of hauling the mail, Mary grew tired. With the help of Sister Amadeus, Mary opened a laundry business in Cascade, Montana.

One afternoon, Mary spotted a cowboy who owed her money.

"Hey, mister!" she shouted. "You owe me for laundry. Now pay up!"

He looked at her and laughed. "You got me mixed up with somebody else," he said, and turned to walk away.

Mary spun him around. "You owe me money," she said, with her six-shooter in her hand.

The surprised cowboy reached into his pocket so fast, he pulled out all the money he had. Mary grabbed it, counted out what he owed her, tucked the rest in his vest pocket, and walked away.

On her eighty-second birthday, Mary Fields was laid to rest at the foot of a mountain trail that leads to the old St. Peter's Mission. It was a road Mary traveled for many years, hauling supplies and mail for a mission and a nun she had loved so well.

Sometimes at night, as the winds blow down that mountain, you can hear thundering hoofbeats, a whip cracking, and a loud voice saying, "Move it!"

That's Stagecoach Mary Fields!